WHY SHOULD I PROTECT NATURE?

BARRON'S

Books in the
WHY SHOULD I? Series:

WHY SHOULD I Save Water?
WHY SHOULD I Save Energy?
WHY SHOULD I Protect Nature?
WHY SHOULD I Recycle?

First edition for the United States and Canada published in 2005
by Barron's Educational Series, Inc.

Published in Great Britain in 2002 by Hodder Wayland, an imprint
of Hodder Children's Books
© Copyright 2002 Hodder Wayland

All inquiries should be addressed to:
Barron's Educational Series, Inc.
250 Wireless Boulevard
Hauppauge, New York 11788
www.barronseduc.com

ISBN-13: 978-0-7641-3154-7
ISBN-10: 0-7641-3154-0

Library of Congress Catalog Card No. 2004109989

Printed in China
9 8 7 6 5 4 3 2

WHY SHOULD I PROTECT NATURE?

Written by Jen Green

Illustrated by Mike Gordon

BARRON'S

Nature is the big, wild world all around us, from giant oak trees to little acorns and wiggling worms.

The birds chirping in the trees are part of nature ...

so is the salty smell of the sea ...

6

splashing in rain
puddles ...

and the soft fur on
a donkey's nose.

Yuck!

or creepy ...

but then our class went on a trip.

9

On our trip, we went to the sea and looked in tide pools. It was great!

On the way home, we had a picnic in a park.

Everyone got a bit rowdy.
Craig and Marina broke
some branches,

I threw my
soda can,

John picked
some flowers,

and Sally
tried to swat
a bee.

Our teacher, Miss Wade, said we should protect nature, not hurt it.

Why should I protect nature?

She asked, "What do you think would happen if everyone broke off branches?"

"The trees would have no leaves left, and they couldn't grow properly. Birds couldn't nest in their branches.

"There would be
        no flowers left,

and we'd have
no honey for
breakfast.

18

And what would happen if we all dropped litter whenever we liked?"

"The countryside would be knee-deep in paper, plastic, and tin cans.

Birds and other animals could choke or get trapped in litter, and die."

21

"Instead of picking flowers, we could plant flowers in a corner of the garden.

Butterflies and bees love flowers, so they'll visit, too."

"We could plant a tree instead of breaking branches.

Cleaning up litter keeps nature looking lovely, and helps animals and birds."

Now we have fun
protecting nature.

28

After all, people are part of nature too!

29

Notes for parents and teachers

Why Should I?

There are four titles about the environment in the *Why Should I?* series: *Why Should I: Save Water? Save Energy? Recycle?* and *Protect Nature?* These books will help young readers to think about simple environmental issues, and other social and moral dilemmas they may come across in everyday life. The books will help children to understand environmental change and how to recognize it in their own surroundings, and also help them to discover how their environment may be improved and sustained. Thinking about recycling will also teach children to consider others and to act unselfishly.

Why Should I Protect Nature? introduces the topic of the environment – the natural world around us, whether we live in a city or the country. It introduces the fact that humans can harm nature, but we can also help to protect it. The book introduces a number of simple tasks that children can carry out to help protect the natural world.

Suggestions for reading the book with children

As you read the book with children, you may find it helpful to stop and discuss issues as they come up in the text. Children might like to reread the story, taking on the role of different characters. Which character in the book reflects their own attitude to nature most closely? How do their opinions differ from those expressed in the book?

The book describes a number of ways in which people can harm nature, including dropping litter, picking flowers, and harming animals and insects. Will anyone admit to doing any of these things? The book discusses the consequences of such actions, especially if everyone were to do the same. Introduce the idea that the natural world is also harmed not only by pollution caused by waste from farms and factories but also from our homes and cities. Pollution may damage the air, water, or the soil under our feet.

30

The end of the book introduces the idea that humans are also part of nature. Like all animals, we need clean air to breathe, water to drink, and space in which to live. Plants and animals provide us with all our food and help to make the world fit to live in. Discuss the idea that we cannot live without the natural world and stress that this is why it is vital that we learn to protect it – for our own as well as nature's sake.

Reading the book and discussing the protection of nature may introduce children to a number of unfamiliar words, including agriculture, environment, extinct, habitat, industry, litter, pollution, recycling. Make a list of all the new words and discuss what they mean.

Suggestions for follow-up activities

Children may have gone on a field trip to the shore or countryside similar to the one described in the book. Encourage them to describe their own experiences and feelings using the book as a framework. They might like to write an account of their trip, or alternatively make up a story about an imaginary visit to the shore or countryside. The stories could be put together to make a book.

The book introduces a number of simple ways in which we can help to protect nature, such as picking up litter and planting a flower garden. Take a trip to the local park to study conditions there, and investigate how humans are helping and harming nature locally. Children might like to create a wild flower area in a corner of the playground or in the garden at home. Other ideas for helping to protect nature include organizing a local litter clean-up, and not using pesticides on the garden. Children might like to build a simple birdhouse or make a small pond for water creatures using an old tub. Do the children have other ideas to help protect the natural world?

Books to read

Amos, Janine. *Pollution*. Orlando, FL: Steck-Vaughn, 1993.
Describes the ways in which our air, water, and soil are being polluted.

Bailey, Donna. *What We Can Do About Conserving Energy*. New York: Franklin Watts, 1992.
Identifies energy conservation issues and gives possible solutions for families and local groups.

Bellamy, David J. *How Green Are You?* New York: Crown Books, 1991.
Provides information and projects about ecology that teach children and their families how to conserve energy, protect wildlife, and reduce pollution.

Berenstain, Stan, and Jan Berenstain. *Berenstain Bears Don't Pollute (Anymore)*. New York: Random House, 1991.
The bears form the Earthsavers Club to teach others how to stop polluting and protect natural resources.

Dorros, Arthur. *Follow the Water from Brook to Ocean*. New York: HarperCollins, 1993.
Follows water from rainfall on the roof to the ocean and explains how important it is to keep our water clean.

Gibbons, Gail. *Recycle! A Handbook for Kids*. New York: Little, Brown & Company, 1996.
Explains the process of recycling from start to finish, focusing on five types of garbage, and describing what happens to each when it is recycled.